words
Epic Poems of a Poetess

words
Epic Poems of a Poetess

Written by:
Lady Melanie Ann Marie Elizabeth Greenwood

Zillionaires Publishing, L.L.C.
Imagination that Entertains

NEW JERSEY

Copyright 2012 by Zillionaires Publishing, L.L.C.
Printed in the United States
Published by Zillionaires Publishing, L.L.C.
Imagination that Entertains

All rights reserved.

ISBN 978-0-9821530-4-8
Library of Congress Control Number: 2012940797

Dedication Page

This book has been in the making a little over four years. The obstacles I have had to endure and overcome have been many. I cannot tell you how many times I have failed. How many times I have been tempted to wave a white flag and simply give up. But through it all, I learned one most valuable lesson about myself and that is I am definitely someone who simply has no patience for dealing with I CAN'T.

So, I would like nothing more than to dedicate this book to YOU. Not telling — but showing — you that no matter what obstacles may find you, no matter how time consumes you, YOU CAN!

Aspiration

Gently knitted into the fabric of my hope
Is my ambition
Every day, aspiration calls my name
Every night, I find myself returning
To that single-most desire – my dream
Every time my purpose surfaces
Procrastination holds me at bay
I do my best
Is the lie that often finds me
Then there is the valence I inhabit
Of my enemy
Jealousy
Along with fear
Constantly nagging me
Still, every day, aspiration calls my name
And willingness
Desperately cutting though the chains
I placed on myself
But it's failure who mocks me
Sitting comfortably
At the edge of my consciousness
But gently knitted into the fabric of my hope
Is my ambition
Tightly guarded by an unfamiliar courage
That inspires me

A Gift

Presented to:

_____

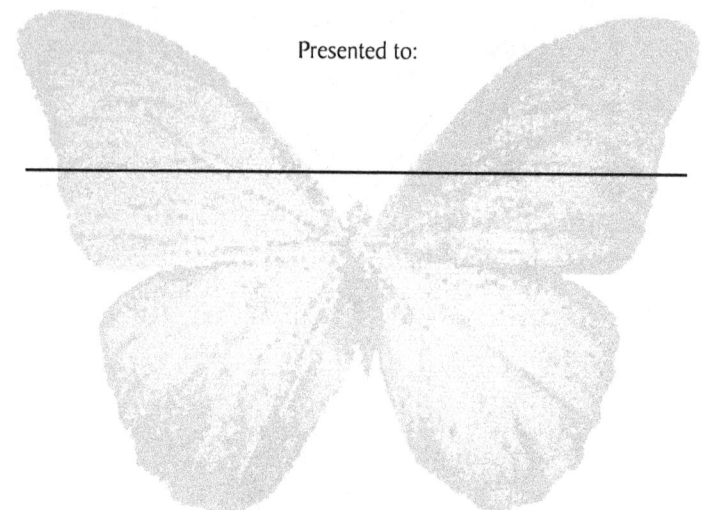

Donations

Thirty Percent of the proceeds from the sales of this book will be divided and donated to the following charities:

- ASPCA® • www.aspca.org
- Avon Foundation • www.avonfoundation.org
- Bell Foundation • www.experiencebell.org
- Christopher and Dana Reeve Foundation® • www.crpf.org
- Feed The Children® • www.feedthechildren.org
- ForSight Vision • www.forsight.org
- Habitat for Humanity® (United States of America/ International)
    • www.habitat.org
- Helen Keller Foundation • www.helenkellerfoundation.org
- Hope Worldwide • www.hopeww.org
- Leg Up Farm • www.legupfarm.org
- Literacy Festival • www.althorp.com
- Make a Wish Foundation® • www.wish.org & www.worldwish.org
- March of Dimes® • www.marchofdimes.com
- Mary Kay Ash Charitable Foundation • www.marykayfoundation.org
- Nelson Mandela Foundation • www.nelsonmandela.org
- New York Cares • www.newyorkcares.org
- Poetry Foundation • www.poetryfoundation.org
- Poetry Society of America • www.poetrysociety.org
- Poets and Writers (Grants and Awards) • www.pw.org
- ProLiteracy Worldwide • www.proliteracy.org
- Saint Jude Hospital • www.stjude.org
- Special Olympics • www.specialolympics.org
- The Fisher House™ Foundation • www.fisherhouse.org
- The Humane Society of the United States/Humane Society
    International • www.humanesociety.org & www.hsi.org
- The Smile Train (Leading Cleft Charity) • www.smiletrain.org
- Wikipedia Foundation® • www.wikipedia.org
- Wounded Warrior Project • www.woundedwarrierproject.org

Acknowledgment

This is my favorite part…

I would like to express my deepest gratitude and admiration to the following individuals without whom this poetry book would not have been possible. May others find the joy I have come to know in all of you.

**YEAH!! FINALLY—IT'S DONE. GREAT JOB EVERYONE!!!!!!
I LOVE YOU ALL!!!!!!!!! TO EVERLASTING FRIENDSHIP!**

To my Designer: Michele Rook
For your unwavering dedication, patience and commitment, especially through my roughest moments. You are a great listener. You really pay attention to what your authors, poets and writers are looking for in their work and, because of that, your creativity is extraordinary. You have been with me from the beginning. Four years, my friend, and I am looking forward to many, many more with you.

Design Avenue
michele.rook@gmail.com
michele@zillionairespublishing.com

To my Editor and Writing Mentor: Marlene Hamerling
You, my dear, have my heart in your hands—for we are nothing without our editors. Special thanks to my very good friend, Amy Harnell, for referring you to me.

M. Hamerling & Associates. Inc.
New York, NY
marlene@hamerlingassociates.com

To my Web Designer: Denmark Francisco
I love what you do and would be lost without you. You make me proud. Cheers to you and your teammates.

Denmark Francisco Marketing
Internet Marketing/Website Designer
www.dsfnyc.com

To my Publicist: Cheryl Duncan
You have taught me the essence—the importance—of a publicist. You are indeed a remarkable woman. Special thanks to Marlene Hamerling for referring you to me.

Cheryl Duncan & Company Inc.
www.cherylduncanpr.com

To my On-Line Publicist: Penny C. Sansevieri
You have introduced me to a whole new world. The Internet! I love the way you bring books to life in videos. You are a genius! Special thanks to About Books for referring you to me.

Author Marketing Experts, Inc.
www.amarketingexpert.com

To my Book Teaser: Sheila English
From the beginning, you've shown such patience and understanding in dealing with my busy schedule. That's how I know I'm in good hands. To you and the entire team: Thank You!

Circle of Seven Productions, Inc.
www.cosproductions.com

To my Photographer: Jack Berman
You are one of my very best friends. To creating beautiful memories through photography! Your talent leaves me both breathless and speechless. I am a huge fan of your work. Brilliant work Jack!

Jack Berman Photograhpy
www.jackberman.com

To my Book Printer: Ryan McMurtry and Yolanda Hall
About Books did me a great service when they referred me to you. And for that, I shall be eternally grateful. Thank you for everything.

Lightning Source
(Printing Press)
www.lightningsource.com

To my Attorneys: David W. Koehser and Richard J. Lambert
Two wonderful attorneys and their extraordinary teams – who led me painlessly through the maze. I am truly blessed.

David W. Koehser
Attorney at Law
www.dklex.com

Richard J. Lambert
Dunn Lambert LLC
Attorneys at Law
www.njbizlawyer.com

<u>Honorary Mentions:</u>
To an everlasting friendship!

About Books, Inc.
www.about-books.com
(Thank you for referring me to Penny, Jeniffer, David and Ryan.)

Jeniffer Thompson, Owner
Monkey C Media
www.monkeyCmedia.com

Pam Lontos
PR/PR Public Relations
www.prpr.net

Nathaniel Lanzer
Account Executive
BookMasters, Inc.
www.bookmasters.com

Beth Eurell
Be Creative Solution
www.becreativesolution.com

To my Mother, Sister, Nephew, Niece, and my very good friends: You are love itself!

To Jackie Arocho: For your understanding of my outrageously creative mind – even if some of my ideas were, at times, a little outside of your reality.

To Quinton Bailey: For that one summer morning at Starbucks on Wall Street. I hope to see your work—when you are ready—published to great success. Congratulations on your new business venture: MyFluffnStuff – www.myfluffnstuff.com

To all those individuals throughout my life, who have influenced it in a positive way, I thank you!

To my life's cheerleaders: For in my darkest moments, you have been and continue to be my light. To show my gratitude, please visit: www.zillionairespublishing.com and click video — Never Ending Star.

I thank God every day for my blessings.

Table of Contents

1. Why the Cover 1
2. My Inspiration 7
    Poet's Inspiration 9
    Sample Poem with Picture 11
3. Bookmark 15
4. Poems
    - A Lifetime 19
    - A Mystery of Awe (Wonder) 20
    - Advocate 21
    - Attitude 22
    - Attraction 23
    - Be 24
    - Beauty 25
    - Becoming 27
    - Betrayal 28
    - Bond 29
    - Book 30
    - Bus Stop 31
    - Chance 32
    - Classic 33
    - Color 34
    - Conceited 35
    - Confront 36
    - Connection 37
    - Curious 38
    - Dangerous 39
    - Deeply 40
    - Déjà Vu 41
    - Discover 42
    - Elegance 43
    - Envy 44
    - Eternity 45
    - Everlasting 46
    - Exclusive 47
    - Exposed 49
    - Fighting 50
    - Flawless Beauty 51
    - Focus 52
    - Freedom 53
    - Generation 54

- Glasses 55
- Glow 57
- Gossiping 58
- Happy Birthday 60
- Heritage 61
- Hope In Silence 62
- Hum 63
- I Am Yours 64
- Imagination 65
- Innocence 67
- Inspiration 68
- Invade 69
- Itself 70
- Journey 71
- Legend 72
- Life 74
- Life Within Yourself 76
- Lovers 77
- Mirror 78
- Moments 79
- Moon 80
- Morning 81
- Muse 82
- My Fairytale Wedding 83
- Ocean Dream 84
- Ordinary 85
- Paper-Doll 86
- Particular 89
- Passionate 90
- Patience 91
- Perceive 92
- Permanent 93
- Photography (Nature) 94
- Playful 95
- Rainbow Full of Dreams 96
- Rebirth 97
- Reflection 98
- Remembrance 100
- Safe 101
- Sailing 102
- Save Me 103
- Save the Date (My Storybook Wedding) 104
- Season's Greetings 105

	- Secure 106
	- Self 107
	- Señorita 108
	- Soul-Mate Friends 109
	- Spontaneous 110
	- Sports 111
	- Strong 112
	- Sun 113
	- Symbol 115
	- Tamed 116
	- Tell 117
	- Timid 118
	- The Artist 120
	- The Engagement 121
	- The Game 122
	- The Heart of One 123
	- The Light 124
	- The Meaning of Christmas 125
	- The Poem of Sorrow 126
	- The Seasons 127
	- True Love 128
	- Unique 129
	- Virgin 130
	- Vision 131
	- Voluptuous 132
	- Walk 133
	- Wedding Bells (The Invitation) 134
	- Wheelchair 135
	- Will You Stay 136
	- Wings of Faith 137
	- You Are 138
5.	Seven Bonus Poems - Dedications 141
	- Brave (dedicated to Mother Teresa) 143
	- Forever - A Letter (dedicated to Princess Diana) ... 144
	- Memories of Me (dedicated to Sergei Grinkov) 145
	- Pennies (dedicated to the Penny) 146
	- Remember Me (dedicated to Selena) 147
	- Shadow (dedicated to Michael Jackson) 148
	- The Towers (dedicated to the Heroes of WTC 9/11) ... 149
	- Within My Touch (dedicated to Helen Keller) 150
6.	The Artist Within (Journal) 153
	- For Your Notes 154, 156, 158, 162
	- For Your Masterpiece 155, 157, 159, 163

7. Special Note of Gratitude — Written by the Poetess 167
8. About the Poetess 168
9. The Remarkable Worldwide Puzzle Board 175
10. A Special Treat — A glimpse of my upcoming novel 179
    - Chapter 1 183

Why the Cover

Why The Cover

For the cover of my poetry book, I wanted something different. Peaceful. But, most of all inspiring.

I'd explained to my designer about thinking outside the box but that I wanted her to think way outside of that box. In fact, I told her the following in my letter to her:

> "I would like you to pull up a chair and have a seat on the moon, look at Earth and everything around it, and use your imagination like you've never used it before. Even if this sound a bit crazy to you, that's fine, still go with it and find a way to make it work. Or, if you feel the need to visit ten or twenty bookstores, take a look at every book cover and just feel what feels right to you. I am a true believer that there is beauty in simplicity. But taking simplicity and making it extraordinary is the key, while still keeping the original beauty of the thing. I hope this makes sense to you."

And at the time, I truly hoped it made sense to her. Because, I know what it's like to walk into a bookstore, look and feel how each cover can inspire you about that particular book. Give you a sense of the story it's dying to tell, as well as a deep insight into the person who wrote it. It is one of the most incredible and wonderful feelings. I'll walk into any bookstore just for that feeling. It's very addictive.

So, when I'd purchased *Jane Austen's – New Edition – Collected and Edited by Deirdre Le Faye*, and read it, there was a letter Jane Austen wrote to her sister Cassandra Austen in 1796. The letter moved me to such a degree that I instructed my designer to read it and told her to do the following, in hopes that it would have done for her what it had so deeply and vividly done for me.

> "Read it once in it's entirety. Then close your eyes and picture the time, place, and anything that comes to mind. Then slowly open your eyes and look at nothing else but the letter itself. And, then read it from beginning to end. But slowly, so as to absorb every letter, every word, every sentence, and every thought that was placed into writing this letter, and I mean the love Jane had for her sister; the joy she felt writing it, the stories, however short, of each individual she spoke of. I want you to absorb everything. What you believe the weather was like, the clothes she wore, the pen and ink she used. Everything! Put yourself in the year 1796. Feel her inspiration. How much she loved writing or maybe even hated it at times. Who knows! And, when you're done, I want you to take that inner extraordinary feeling and know that that is what I want captured on the cover of my poetry book. Work your magic!!!"

My Inspiration

Poet's Inspiration
Written by the Poetess

While I am inspired by everything around me, I find that the majority of my inspiration comes from looking at paintings or pictures. A perfect example would be as if you were looking at a magic eye. If you have never done it, I highly recommend doing so.* It's a wonderful experience. So, in essence, that is how I see when I look at things. At first it's abstract and then, it opens itself to me.

Enjoy!

---

* Visit Wikipedia® (The Free Encyclopedia) for the definition and type in Magic Eye at www.wikipedia.org.

Goddesses

Beneath an immortal sun
Roses bloom into colorful quilts
Leaves of green – chased by twirling winds
In a nearby pond – a school of fish
Surfaces – to catch a glimpse of divinity
Sparrow's chirp in sweet delight
While honey bees greedily feast
On luscious fragrances
Nature admiring – in all its endearment
This day is content – to worship you
Where goddesses dwell
Beneath an immortal sun
In a majestic garden – called Eden

The Poet

A poet —
I call myself
Not knowing what it means

I am just someone
In love with words
That's all it really is

I look at things
- without request -
They spill themselves to me
And the only way to communicate
Is to write for you to read

But every time
I start to write
The words just seem to rhyme

And every time
I try to rhyme
The words just scream out—crime

It's a never-ending saga
Between myself and I
So I call myself
- a poet -
Indeed—it's a fine line

But I figure
If I keep believing it
One day I just may be
As good as that man called Shakespeare
What a joy that would be

Melanie Greenwood
©2012 Zillionaires
Publishing, L.L.C.

www.zillionairespublishing.com

Lady Melanie Ann Marie Elizabeth Greenwood

Poems

A Lifetime

The Anniversary

You are still the calming presence in my life
My Lady
You are still as beautiful as ever
From our first steps
   courting
   the engagement
     to I do
You've never stopped being you – my true love
My love for you still grows
   with each waking day
Each night
   my dreams are filled with sweet thoughts of you
For you
I would give anything
Do everything
You give so much of yourself to me
I am blessed
To know you are my wife and I am your husband
A lifetime of discovering
The best parts of ourselves

A Mystery Of Awe (Wonder)

Every new day holds
a mystery of awe,
when I look at him.
A message in each smile!
A puzzle in each word!
With him my days are never dull.
And my anticipation grows.
But patience I must learn –
Forget patience –
Truth be told,
I cannot wait for tomorrow, my love.

Lady Melanie Ann Marie Elizabeth Greenwood

Advocate

A Grand Gesture
— Powerful
 — Compelling

I take pleasure
In what I do
 — For you

Your knowingness momentarily hidden
is expressed in your being

The speaker of my voice
 — within my voice

For there lies
 — unhidden truth Outspoken

My name is
 Melanie

And yes
 — I am your Advocate

Attitude

From my standpoint

My attitude
Is never really
A problem

Because –
I always get my way

Attraction

The recipe of attraction

Begins with…
1 Drop Eternal Essence
2 Cups Purity
¼ Teaspoon Aromatics (Heated Fragrance)
5 Ounces Charm
1 Zest of Appeal
Indulgence
Perfectly Ripe
One Large
1 ½ Cups Adoration
– gently mixed with Style
2 Splashes Enchantment
An Ounce of Bitter-Sweet
A Hint of Timeless Extract
(measured precisely is the key)
Approximately…
3 Pints Hidden Secret
4 Slices of Desire
Remember to Add Allure
– they're the secrets to the eyes

Those ingredients…
Creating fascinations
– will be the icing that entices

Pleasing to the senses
Tasteful delights
Placed in a bottle
(the Power of Attraction)
A Fragrance of Unlimited Pleasures
The Very Essence of You
Perfectly Complete!

Be

This can't *be*
– all there is to life

Beauty

See me
        Beauty
Frozen in time and space
Becoming an eloquent memory
Sort of
        a keepsake
For you to proclaim
Your vision of grace
But I am
        looked upon
                by ugliness
Speaking
        only to reform me
Over crowding
        with jealousy
Captured by desires
        of destruction
And you
        who think
                it is preservation
You sleeping beauty
With your eyes
                wide open –
                          see nothing
But yet
        I remain
                frozen in time and space
For those pure hearts
                    who
                          blind their eyes
                          disarm their hate
                          open their minds
                          listen in silence
                          For just a while

Then…
        beauty reveals itself
To those wanting eyes
With an open heart
Who know
Don't question
              Beauty
                    See me

Becoming

It was only in
Becoming
A child again
– that I found me

Betrayal

Your camouflage
        is the very skin you wear
Portraying innocence
        in a very bewitching way
Turning trust
        into a disease
Hurting
        Destroying
                you take pleasure in
Rendering blindness
        where light once existed
Soulless
        Heartless
Revenging
        is your only deed
Yet somehow
        in that vindictive mind of yours
You see yourself as blameless
        for all pain
The truth
        (should it be told)
You would kill innocence
        to save yourself
                the embarrassment
                      that is you
Born to betray
        is your only belief
And…
        My only wish
                is that we never meet

Lady Melanie Ann Marie Elizabeth Greenwood

Bond

My favorite time of day
Is stripping my mind
Of its judgmental clothing

Bare – completely nude
The core of my purity
Returns itself to creation

Quieted – I listen
Immersed in the memory
Of my true self
Raw memories flow
From everyone – everything
– a telepathic connection –

Reminded of my spiritual freedom
And the covenant of my bond
– to protect
Everyone – everything
– including –
My naked mind

Book

One of the greatest
Books ever given to me

Is the one I've always had
And never read
                – me

Bus Stop

Standing in line at the bus stop...

A stranger asked, "How do I impress someone like you?"

"You already did." I told him and turned away.

Then, he asked, "Aren't you curious?"

"About what?" I rudely replied.

He said, "How you could impress me?"

Surprised, I cleared my mind and looked at him with a pair of naked eyes. Smiling, I looked up at the sky and at the traffic passing by. I looked down, checking for the time and smiled. Play date between the wind and tree leafs began exactly at five. While strangers pretended they were wide awake, bright, and alive. I looked at him – this stranger – and smiled. Then asked, "Why?"

My bus came and I got aboard. I met a gentleman who brushed the seat next to him and smiled. I huffed and puffed, rolling my eyes. Debating whether to sit or pass him by. He patted the seat a few more times. I sat... <u>wondering why</u>.

He held my hand. It warmed my heart. I whispered, "I won't cry."

"Footprints in the sand," he replied.

My bus took off. I smiled.

Chance

On the edge of time
    chance stands
        and lends itself to me

With a whispering wind
    echoing stories
        of what tomorrow will bring

A hope that chance
    will guide your path
        to return you back to me

Where loves remains
    still echo in
        that once familiar place

Where chance awaits
and history can begin

Lady Melanie Ann Marie Elizabeth Greenwood

Classic

From what point of view
    What angle
        Do I explain you?
You are someone
    Who just stands there
With one expression
    And that is you
        Classic
No multitude of characteristics
No endless explanation
Simplicity
       Is the only conclusion
Simple colors
     – Please
No abstract art
Keep the vision true
       Tamed
No changes required
No guessing
No placing indiscretions
       Of any kind
I'll tell you
    What to do
I am classic
One of a kind
    Easy
        Natural
            I flow in a straight line
I go on and on
      For quite a while
           Never ending
I am tradition
     – Actually
Where events
      Bow to please me
Classic
      Isn't it
          Me
              – We never die

Color

You are color:

A forceful speaker
An action – of its own voice
An exotic tribal dancer
Swaying in many directions
With drums beating – colorful messages
A lover – tasting colors

Interesting
   – your character

Conceited

What is it like
    To be me
Over the top
    Literally
Point of excellence
    That would be me
Your inspiration
    I'd have it
        No other way
Perfection
    In every way
Opinion
    Only my own
        Really matters
Ambition
    What do you think
        (sarcastically)
Loyalty
    Only to myself
Grace
    I keep
Celebrate
    I do it every day
Fashion
    Look at me
    (sarcastically)
Conviction
    Whose
        Mine or mine
Laughter
    Who's got time
Immortality
    I'm smiling
        inside

Confront

I think –
You should make a decision
About how to respond to me
Either be nice – or mean
But come to some agreement
With yourself –
With regards to you and me
I'm actually tired
Of dying my hair
Covering the multitude of grays
I know my mistakes
And full responsibility – I take
But – it is not your job
This constant degrading of me
From childhood to now
This roller coaster
Of admiration and disgrace
Is simply – more of a nuisance – to me now
But truth be told
I wonder – what it is you secretly hold
For no one holds – this long – such hate
Confront your demons
For even you have them, my dear
And just may be
You'll finally find happiness
In the short time
You have left here
So please – make a decision
In regards to you and me
Prove – once and for all
Your word is something
You can keep

Lady Melanie Ann Marie Elizabeth Greenwood

Connection

No one knows me
Better than nature
Who toys with me
Like a puppet
Determining…
My ever
      — changing moods

Curious

A rarity
    tantalizing
        tempting
Wanting to know
    show me
        tell me
            I want to grow
To take this new knowledge
    arouse my senses
        give it a name
            this unknown
Feed me
    Feed me
        the fruit of knowledge
Teach me
    don't leave me alone
Dying
    in my insane hunger
You
    remaining a mystery
        remaining unknown
Curious
    Curious
        I want to know
Learn
    Grow
        Specialize –
            Make you my own

Lady Melanie Ann Marie Elizabeth Greenwood

Dangerous

Look at you –
Trying to read me
With fear – seeping
Through your very pores
Your stale approach
– bores me
Smelling your desperation
– to amuse me
Believing your invitation
– to tempt me
A willing sacrifice
Foolish
I have no desire
– to taste you
But be careful
– don't wake me
I am dangerous
Make no mistake
In your assumption

Body language
– is my specialty

Deeply

Tears each night
Is what she does
Before she sleeps
To change a past
She never lived
Except – to feel deeply

Deja Vu

In this place
I feel a heightened sense of awareness
Familiarity tapping on my consciousness
History revealing a previous experience
Unknown – this experience seems new
Reliving my Déjà Vu

Discover

Against a light gray wall
My silhouette takes form

Against a light white wall
Angelic wings clothe me

Against a light silver wall
I sparkle like rare jewelry

Against a light black wall
Beauty finds me

Against a light cream wall
I blend in quite well

Against a light tan wall
I radiate in stillness

Combined – under a soft white light
I discovered – a Portrait of Myself

Elegance*

Poor – am I
With hands
That bear no rings

My clothes – ill fitting
A shield of invisibility

My hair – my nails
Improper things

My face – drained
Filled with shadows
Blocking – a sun full of promises

Coil – is the daily life I live
But I find –
I am open to the idea of elegance
Desperately aching
– to honor my nobility

Coil: Anything wound in circles or in a spiral.

Envy

Look at the cliché
        False impression
                Fabricated lies
                        To seem special
Claiming the
        Know-it-all
                Attitude
Miss Illusion – fooled

Suffocated thinking
        Fancy this
                Fancy that

Embracing her own silhouette

Goddess like pretending

What sickness
        Is she believing

Uninspiring
        Undeserving
                Intentional
                        Just to be liked

Believing she is achieving
        (what exactly!)

Undeserving vision
        Nobody cares to listen

Who are you anyway?

My name is
        Envy –
                I'll listen

Lady Melanie Ann Marie Elizabeth Greenwood

Eternity

How miraculous a gift,
when two souls are meant to be.
Created by the hands
of extraordinary originality.

One soul divided,
released and reunited.
A union that was blessed,
before the soul was divided.

And through a world of calamity
You have found the greatest gift,
and proved that true love really does exist.

So…
Upon the day you stand together,
under God's unity.
May angels guide your memory
to that special place in heaven,
where you both found ETERNITY.

Everlasting

Our once-in-a-lifetime has arrived
You are my Husband and I am your Wife
I love you and you love me
In your presence, I am speechless
    And you are speechless in mine
Together
This is our beginning
This moment will be remembered
As the day I placed my life in your hand
    And you placed yours in mine
Knowing it will be everlasting

Exclusive

You are
   your own philosopher

A decision maker

You truly believe
   in your ability
      to do
         to have
            to become
               anything
                  you desire

Knowledge
  and
Understanding

Have given you
   your power

Applauding your confidence
   comes naturally
And…
Your knowingness
   is where your certainty lies

To you
   excuses are the myths
      others choose to live by
But…
   The laws that govern you

Have taught you
   to humble yourself

Belonging to no one
   but yourself

You are what
   I aspire to

Becoming a leader
   in my own rights

Belonging only to
   myself

Humbling myself
   by the laws
      that govern me

Choosing to no longer
   live by the
      myths you consider
         excuses

Knowing that
   my certainty lies in
      my knowingness

Naturally applauding
   my confidence

Finding my power
   in
Knowledge
   and
Understanding

Taking my desires
   To become
      To have
         To do
            Anything

Making decisions
Being my own philosopher
   Becoming
      Exclusive

Lady Melanie Ann Marie Elizabeth Greenwood

Exposed

Standing –
In the middle
Of a stage
– exposed –

The irony
– empty seats

Fighting

Live for me
Taste for me
Explain these
Things for me
While I fight
  – to survive

Introduce me
Tell me
What's familiar for you
Is foreign to me

Happiness…what is –
Sorry for the incomplete sentences
But I have so much to learn
  – so much to give

But at the moment
While I am fighting
  – to survive
I need you
  – to live for me

Flawless Beauty

Every soul
Exudes a flawless beauty
Intelligence in each expression
Silent grace it uses
Gliding with each step
Attention draws and blinds the sight
Of those eyes with evil intentions
But those who seek true beauty
See only the truth, then smile
For within a soul lives only perfection
Who calls itself Flawless Beauty

Focus

It requires focus
To do what I do
Everyday – constant
– no breaks –
Except to refocus
My sometimes wandering mind
– simple adjustments –
Worth enduring
For the permanent taste
Of accomplishment
And truly
What is life
If not for focus
– my favorite word

Freedom

I am freedom
in a frame
Born from imagination
an artist's creation
I am colors
dancing in water
for your delightment
A reminder
for your memory
of lasting impressions
I am unlimited potential
of a dreamer's reality
I am yours –
Embrace me
Delight me
Enjoy me
See your freedom
within me
I am freedom
in a frame
I am free

Generation

I am bounded
By my name
– Generation

Glasses

How!

How do I write a poem
    on a blank page
        that is already there

It is a feeling
    a knowing
        a Story

It is wearing
    3D glasses
        in a movie
            that already exists

That unseen blur

    between

        your eyes

        and

        the screen

Seeing
    it's true form

Becoming a part
    and yet
        hidden

It is an experience
    on such a deeper level

It is enhanced
Magnified

Except –
    While others
        can remove these glasses – at will

Permanent – are the glasses I wear

Glow

Did you ever wait
In the mist of a night
Covered by a moonlight
So bright – you glowed

Gossiping*

well – the gossip is…
you know *who*
had several plus words to say
about you know *what*

that *what*
was caught several times
fluffing you know whose feathers

i have to assume
that's what got *who* started
with the several words
to say about you know *what*

the scoop is…
who was caught cheating
searching in   you know *what*
…for new words

something about wanting to cause
a greater effect – on *what*
since – you know *who*
didn't finish you know what
but…you can't tell *who* that

which I heard
is exactly what – *what* did
hence being caught several times
fluffing – you know *who's* feathers

causing – you know
…*who* having several words to say
but…*what*…I heard…just laughed
which i'm sure was bound to have
who – plucking feathers

Lady Melanie Ann Marie Elizabeth Greenwood

words — Epic Poems of a Poetess

last I heard…
there was some gluing of feathers
whether it was *who* or *what*
no one seems to know
only speculations
tid bits…here and there

i think it's *who*
but…you didn't hear it from me.

Note: This poem was written looking at a photograph of two ducks who looked as if they truly were gossiping. I had so much fun writing it.

Happy Birthday

I thought the first thing you saw
On your special day
   Was me
See, that smile right there
Is what I knew I would see
   From you
You melt my heart, you know
For your birthday, I wanted to melt yours
I love you
You know how I know that
Because you're the only one
I would wear this birthday hat for

Lady Melanie Ann Marie Elizabeth Greenwood

Heritage

I am well grounded
A woman of my heritage
A legacy filled with culture
My birthright
   delicate treasures
      passed down through tradition
         native to my beliefs
Wealthy is my inheritance
Built on a foundation
Of ancestral teachings
My future is certain…
        because of my heritage

Hope In Silence

You should know…
For every struggle you endured
For every weakness you witnessed
For every argument you resolved
For every stubbornness, you showed patience
For every teardrop, you lent understanding
For every threat to quit, you listened
For every step taken, you encouraged
For every triumph you experienced
For every hour
For every minute
For every second, of every day
You have always done one thing—never given up
You were then—you are now and always will be—my hope in silence

Lady Melanie Ann Marie Elizabeth Greenwood

Hum

I hum and hum
And hum and hum
Humming as I go
To only hum and hum
– some more
I hummed – an entire row
Like row and row
I hum and hum
– knowing nothing more
I hum and hum
And hum and hum
Humming – running home
I entered – with one final hum
– humming never more

I Am Yours

His face radiates beauty.
Unmarked! Untouched!
His lips a forbidden fruit —
Yet, I desire them.

The softness of his hair,
calls the tips of my fingers,
that they tremble,
at the very thought of touch.

But, it is his eyes
Alluring! Showing!
Telling a story
that beckons and consumes
my every thought.
I give in freely.
No spoken words needed,
I am yours.

Lady Melanie Ann Marie Elizabeth Greenwood

Imagination

At half past six – one eve
I stood silently on a pier
Where I came to put to rest
The mystery that happened there

The mystery claimed
At precisely six
Not one minute before or past
Whosoever touch the sea
– on good Friday
A mermaid ye will be

So I braced myself
At the stroke of six
My trembling finger touched the sea
Immediately – I sprung a tail
And fell – head first
Into the deep blue sea

Before regret
Could settle in
I kissed my life goodbye
Then sunk beneath
The water's surface
Embracing this new life of mine

My tail took
A little getting used to
But I learned to swim again
Then quickly – with high hopes
I set out – to find the place
Where mermaids dwell

I swam and swam – eagerly
With dolphins on my tail
In search of Atlantis
I rode a huge wave there

Putting to rest another mystery
As the gates to Atlantis welcomed me
I heard a distant echo
Someone calling out to me
With a couple of blinks
I turned and looked
My father stood – with a cross look

Confused – I looked down
Sure enough – I found two legs, two feet –
Ten wiggling toes
Which stood firmly on the ground
Sudden laughter burst out of me
Further tickling my funny bone and shaking
Every part of me

Fear had stopped my delirious theory
And the use of my imagination
Leaving me just a little bit dreary.

IMAGINATION –
One ought to be thankful
For such a thing.

Lady Melanie Ann Marie Elizabeth Greenwood

Innocence

Mesmerizing
    Observation
Blameless
    No judgment here
Overpowering presence
Reflecting
    Adoration
        Greatness
            Respect
You are a danger
    No one
        Must embrace
Shadows haunt you
    To claim you
        To break you
To delight in your losing
    Your childlike image
        Your childlike sensibility
Yet you remain grounded
By your innocence
Your honesty
    Protects you
        From
            Self

Inspiration

You possess a quiet confidence
A delicate insight into your purpose for life
A subtle assurance in your way of thinking
A revelation that arouses creativity
And a gentle optimism within your motivation to inspire

Invade

It's rather ironic
That like an intruder
I am constantly invading
  – my own thoughts

Itself

The Greatest and Deepest Secret…

   I Keep…

        Is…

            Itself…

No Other Explanation Needed

Journey

I journey daily
Unconscious of the trip
Blinded by my routine
Which never changes

Staring at familiar strangers
In the wee hours of dawn
And again
With a setting sun
That's bored with seeing me

But still I journey
With forgotten dreams
Seldom wondering
If hope ever existed

Forgetting my name
I journey on
Knowing today
I may suddenly decide
That a wrong train
Is what is needed

Changing my routine
I journeyed today
On a whole new path
Smiling the whole way

Legend

How do you know a Legend?

Is it the mother –
    who defends her child when bullies attack

Is it the father -
    who is willing to endure unconstructive criticism
        to appear brave for his wife and child

Is it the teacher -
    spending her last dime
        missing three meals a day
            to purchase the materials she needs to inspire her students

Is it the waitress -
    who works
        double
            triple shifts
                to feed the homeless in her neighborhood

Is it the bus driver -
    who would allow his paycheck to be deducted funds
        for those who think nothing of stealing a free ride

Is it the firefighter-
    police officer
        soldier
            neighborhood watchman
                security guard
                      the unsung heroes
                          who wake up everyday
                              making sure their families
                                  their little legends are cared for
                                    - just in case they don't come home

Is it the doctor -
    who spends countless years and money
        to perfect the art of saving lives

Lady Melanie Ann Marie Elizabeth Greenwood

words — Epic Poems of a Poetess

Is it the man -
    who picks up your garbage while you sleep
        who silently thanks you
            because you took the time to place that one tin can
                in the right bin
                    and smiles because he found another person
                    who cares about the environment
                    as much as he does
                        and you made his night

Is it the baker -
    who every morning at 4:00 a.m.
        in pure joy wakes up knowing
            that today he will bake your bagel better than he did yesterday
            all because he loves the gratitude in your smile
                when you take that first bite

Is it the person -
    who still remembers
        what his or her mother said about
            helping an elderly person cross the street
              - and does it

So, how do you know a Legend?

By the many good deeds a person does in their lifetime

Some might argue otherwise

But the fact remains
    ordinary people
        do extraordinary things
           - indeed -

And you inspire me

Life

You are…
    A zillion chances
        Of remembrance
    A zillion chances
        Of calm enlightenment
    A zillion chances
        Of inspired certainty
    A zillion chances
        Of flawlessness

You are…
    A zillion chances
        Of magnificent stillness
    A zillion chances
        Of silent boldness
    A zillion chances
        Of untarnished persona
    A zillion chances
        Of eloquent possibilities

You are…
    A zillion chances
        Of elegant existence
    A zillion chances
        Of desired mystery
    A zillion chances
        Of untamed visions
    A zillion chances
        Of questionable truth

Lady Melanie Ann Marie Elizabeth Greenwood

You are…
    A zillion chances
        Of spirited muse
    A zillion chances
        Of awakened interruption
    A zillion chances
        Of unbearable honesty
    A zillion chances
        Of timeless clichés

You are…
    A zillion chances
        Saying…(fill in the blank)

You are…
    A zillion chances
        Saying – Hello Life

Life Within Yourself

Sometimes it's all about
 keeping memories
But most of the time
 it's about change

Tell your story
Keep your memories
Most importantly…
 Discover life
   – within yourself.

Lady Melanie Ann Marie Elizabeth Greenwood

Lovers

Pure – a moment in itself
When the gentle touch
– of love takes hold
Never letting go
Emotions swell
In places where love dwells
That image of affliction
Finds me losing time
But like sweet Nectar
Nourishing everything
Melting away
 – your lover is here to stay

Mirror

Bright
Full of passion and conviction
Boundaries mean nothing to you
Normal routines are beneath you
Success mirrors you
You don't dream – you do
Your convictions – open to view
– not review
One could hurt themselves
– thinking for you
Too powerful – even for you
No one should aspire to be you
Not even you
But I admire you
An imitation of you - a mirror

Moments

Life's many changes
From birth to aging
A lifetime of dreaming
Dreams lingering somewhere
   between hopes and wishes
      shadowed by fear
         explained as excuses
Forecasting
Someday
   when the planets align
      and the timing is right
         your star will shine bright
But life's many changes
Are constant reminders
Of a lifetime of dreams
Still lingering somewhere
Between hopes and wishes
Singing
They are your
Defining moments

Moon

If you took a walk in time
To when the world began
You would realize
The moon was there
And you held me
– in your hand

Morning

Somewhere after dawn
Before the setting of a full moon
I dream of morning

Uninterrupted stillness
Nature's work of art
Inspiring creativity
Waking my inner muse

Swimming in still water
My mind explodes
Scattering reality
Hovering in fantasy

Breaking rules
Caught in the junction
Of lingering moments
Questioning – how do I cheat time
Remaining in morning

Muse

Timeless – is where you live
Effortlessly fitting into
Past – present – future
Never changing – only inspiring
Unforgettable songs – Tasteful dance
Memorable dreams – Magnificent poems
Timeless books – Exquisite paintings
Pieces of you, in everything
  Influencing
    Creating
      Never imposing
You are
A well-known secret
Hidden silently
In the shadows of my existence
Inspiring me!

Lady Melanie Ann Marie Elizabeth Greenwood

My Fairytale Wedding*

I thought days like this
Were only meant for storybooks
For I never dreamt
My special day with you
Would be called a fairytale
But here I am and there you are
Among families and friends

Thank you for sharing with us
My fairytale
For being a part of my storybook wedding

* Note: This poem was a wedding invitation.

Ocean Dream

He will lure you into his senses
And capture you with his touch
He promises you serenity
The peace you have been longing for

He will embrace you with his warmth
While silently he speaks to your heart
Providing you with security
And quenching your inner thirst

But while he caresses you slowly
He is studying your every part
To make sure he does not lose you
And the work he has done so far

Once your mind has opened
To understanding his world
Then he teaches you
How not to fear
Leaving you with the promise of knowing
That he will always be near

So tonight when you close your eyes
And feel you are drifting away
There will be no reason to fear
For he is reminding you of his love
By giving you an Ocean Dream

Ordinary

I meet extraordinary
– every day
Those who keep themselves
– ordinary
Out of fear
– I use to be extraordinary

Paper-Doll

I still remember
    The exact spot
        I once called
            My home

Part of…
    A magnificent tree
        An original
            A whole

Which became
        Little pieces

Sold
        Around the globe

Parts were used
    For many different things

Some of which
    Built homes

While others
    Were burned
        To create a flame
            Bringing warmth

I was used
    To express myself
        In a much more
            Elegant way

Placed on the floor
    Of a studio
        Run by a designer
            Named Faith

Lady Melanie Ann Marie Elizabeth Greenwood

words — Epic Poems of a Poetess

Talented
    Were the creative hands
        That drew
            Every inch of me

Line by line
    I came to life

My curves
    Took form
        Fingers
            Toes
                She drew it all

The height of
    A life-size doll

Then ruffled
    My edges
        So delicately

As she cut
    Along my curves
        And glued me
            To a cardboard

Tall – I stood
    Once more

Then piece by piece

    Her masterpiece

The famous wedding dress
    Was born

The final touch
    Was a vintage veil
        Diamonds
            Tiara
                — I wore it all

It became
    The crown
        A princess wore

That is the story
    Of the paper-doll trail

An extraordinary tree
    Became the doll
        That wore the dress

A lady wore
    on that special day
        that history remembers

The lady
The Princess
    on her Wedding Day

Lady Melanie Ann Marie Elizabeth Greenwood

Particular*

A delicious taboo
My fastidious ways
Your venom
  – my paradise

---

* Fastidious: Excessively particular, critical, or demanding; hard to please.

Passionate

It's an oddity –
That I should have such
Strong passionate passion
– for nothing

Patience

A desperate twinkle
– of ocean blue
Fragile expression
Foreshadowing –
Smiles of joy
Downward lips –
And fallen drops of rain
Across rosy cheeks
That never seem to fade
Hiding – insignificant – a thing
For fear – of fear
And other things
Silently hoping – somewhere
A little patience – if you dare

Perceive

Truthfully – I wonder
In the mixture of things
How this sordid foolishness
– Perceives

Permanent

The way you inspire me
Is filled with so much love
I lose myself so deeply
– I ache – permanently!

Photography (Nature)

Elements – natural things
Environment – both wild and calm
Morning Light – darkness falls
Black and White – colors
Creating mystery…
A photographer's playground

Playful

My diversions –
are the amusement park
– of my life

Fondly playing –
in the sandbox
– of my day

I constantly amuse myself

Playfulness is key
It is after all
– who I am

Rainbow Full of Dreams

Upon the dawn of each new day,
angels whisper in your ear.
Listen softly to your heart,
it will guide your eyes to see,
the signs that mother nature leaves.
A trail for those who dare believe
in love's true heart and destiny.
You shall always find, within a drop of rain
that falls out of the sky,
will reveal the face of the man you long to meet.

So follow that rainbow full of dreams,
you hold so dear for you and him,
that no pot of gold could ever buy,
the blessing sent from the Divine.

At the other end
of your rainbow full of dreams,
angels whisper in his ear
listen softly to his heart,
guiding him to see
the signs that mother nature left behind,
a trail for those who dare believe
in heart's true love and destiny.
And within a single raindrop,
would reveal that special woman he longed to meet,
which led him to the rainbow full of dreams,
he held so dear for you and him,
that no pot of gold could ever buy
the blessings sent by the Divine.
Here two hearts, which form one soul,
Here their dreams would all unfold.
Because two hearts dare to believe
in heart's true love and destiny.

Lady Melanie Ann Marie Elizabeth Greenwood

Rebirth

The temptations of yesterday
Cleverly finding new ways
For me to carry on today – as if it were yesterday
Reliving stale mistakes – while dreaming of change
Outsmarted
   I carried on today
     As I did yesterday
        While dreaming of change
Then… tomorrow came
And I cleverly found a new way
To outsmart the temptations of yesterday
By living today – as if it were tomorrow
I made the changes – I dreamt of yesterday
Finding my new beginning
A rebirth
I'm looking forward to reliving
Tomorrow's joys
From today

Reflection

Aaaahhhh…

Reflection

Ignore
    Self-Confrontation

Blame
    your Causation
        on a Nation

To save
    your Reputation
        by imitation

Still…
    Procrastination

Claiming
    Victimization

Avoiding
    Responsibility

Effect
    The Offspring
        of Causation

So…
    History
        Repeating
            through Tradition

Teaching
        as a tool of
            Hatred and Conviction

Lady Melanie Ann Marie Elizabeth Greenwood

Instead of Growth
    and Self-Realization

To save a nation
    by Cooperation

For Future Generations
    To witness
        Create and live by
            a New Tradition

But first…
    Begin with…
        Self-Reflection

            That is your…
                Foundation

Remembrance

Exuding inspiration
Where solitude is my indulgence
Walking through moments in time
    that do not yet exist
Reflection of whispering gratitude
Recalling my passionate muse
Radiating harmony
    my mortality
Hidden…
By this never-ending
    weave of skin
        I wear carelessly
My memory
    is letters to myself
Leaving me speechless
Questioning my existence
    I'm not afraid
        I welcome it
            openly
My drug
    is my remembrance
Its effect
    speechlessness

Safe

I love looking at you
– Soundless –
In the invisible
Hidden by perceptions
That at this moment
– Escape me –
Believing you're unseen
Dancing on the surface
Of a most favorable dream
Half awake – half asleep
– unaware –
The invitation – to invite myself in
But I love looking at you
Guarded – defended – protected
Vulnerably – looking at me
From the visible – where it's safe!

Sailing

Sailing
Fresh air filled with a rewarding clarity
Soothing ripples
Cool wind
Self-possessed tranquility
Discovering new emotions
Nature expressing a calm serenity
Exploration filled with endless destinations

Lady Melanie Ann Marie Elizabeth Greenwood

Save Me

I view the world
As one big ocean
I find I'm floating in

To my right is Life

To my left is Death

At front – a complete blur
And darkness stands behind me

Below my feet a deep dark pit
One could quickly slip in

But above I see
This beautiful light
That keeps shining on me
Telling me
You must look up more often
To clear the blur you see
For if you remember
It was I – who first taught you – to breathe

Save the Date

My Storybook Wedding

The rumors are true
The secret is out
We're getting married

Our wedding planner
Is hard at work

His tux is being fitted
And my dress is being taken in
The Maid of Honor and Bridesmaids have been chosen
The wedding cake is sure to be delicious
The main entrée will be chicken, salmon or steak
Drinks are free
   All night
The bachelor party has been cancelled
The Best Man and Groomsmen are still sulking
But the bridal shower is a go
   Male dancers arriving on time
      With treats and plenty of surprises
The bride to be – simply overwhelmed with joy
Now all we need to complete
The perfect storybook wedding
Is confirmation of our guest list
Make sure to save the date
For we guarantee it will be a day to remember

Lady Melanie Ann Marie Elizabeth Greenwood

Season's Greetings

A little bit of everything
This Holiday Season

Crackling noise of paper
With colors of the rainbow
Carefully wrapped around
– precious gifts

Designing Holiday Cookies
Served with…
Warm chocolate milk
Over a cozy fire

While children hold tightly
To soft winter mittens
And the patter of tiny little feet
    Running off to the chimney
        To roast yummy marshmallows

This Holiday Season
A little bit of everything
As families gather
For the season of giving

Secure

Secure
    I am
Knowledge…
        where understanding
                is the key
That secure
      is born first
            within
Only then
      your illumination
           glows
Understand –
      the world outside
Results –
      of the world inside
Secure
      develops wisdom
It knows truth
            never lies
Honesty…
      another key to self-realization
Confronting becomes
    your best friend
Independence…
      it proclaims
Life –
      where none existed
You want secure –
              I see
Start with you
      is what I know
Then illuminate
      your glow
Place judgment aside
Certainty relies
      not on wondering why
Secure
    I am
            Indeed
I say so –
      that's Why

Lady Melanie Ann Marie Elizabeth Greenwood

Self

I am woven
By such fragile threads
Constantly spitting
Millions of personalities
Like misguided branches
Unsure of myself.

Senorita

Leonardo's Mona Lisa
This Modern Senorita
A Picturesque
Fetching an ornament
To adorn the wall
Of my favorite room

Soul-Mate Friends

High fiving
Hips shaking
Eyes blinking
Nose touching
Both laughing
We couldn't decide

Toes wiggling
Knees dancing
Body shaking
Eyes squinting
Both laughing
But we couldn't decide

Running and jumping
Hands embracing
Loudly screaming
Sister – brotherhood
Both laughing
Still – we couldn't decide

Tears flowing
Bear hugging
Well wishing
Both moving
Future awaiting
Joyful feeling
Separate ways
But – a phone call away

Eyes meeting
Memories resurfacing
Warm smiling
Both deciding

A pinkie promise
Toe-tip touching
Symbolizing
Our unbreakable bond

Secretly agreeing
– soul-mate friends

Spontaneous

DELUSION... The Idea!
EXCURSION... The Obstacles!
COMRADE... The Strangers!
ACTUALITY... The Work of Art!
MY DREAM... A Mirage! — UNEDITED!!!

Lady Melanie Ann Marie Elizabeth Greenwood

Sports

The Adrenaline
The Excitement
The Determination to Obtain the Unattainable
The Unwavering Spirit to Persevere
No Limits
The Willpower to Retain Your Commitment
The Achievement that Follows
Persistence
Sports Is the Unthinkable

Strong

The strength of a woman:

A child –
Will live through
Her entire childhood
Never realizing one thing

A girl –
Will live through
Her entire teenage years
Still – never realizing one thing

A woman –
Will live through
Her entire life
Never knowing one thing

How strong she truly is

Sun

The sun
> Hidden Secret
>> From seeing eyes

You found your way on earth

Pleasure
> Up close and personal

A blind man's dream

So – Tell me Sun
What's it like
> Taking human form?

A first for me
> – human
>> You're gifted indeed

Why wait for an Eclipse?
(The Blind man asked)

I desire the experience
> – Not the Kill

You see…
> My time is up
This candle's light
> is burning out
…For the care
> …You've shown the earth
>> (I See)

But tell me
> – Blind man

What do you see?
> When you look at me

Well –
        I look forward
                To these eclipse as well
              (the blind man said)

Truly –
        It's the only time
                      I see
                              (both Laughing)

Lady Melanie Ann Marie Elizabeth Greenwood

Symbol

Never wonder
About your solitude
Dismiss or curse
Its existence
Or the loneliness
That fills the air around you
– instead –
Breathe deep
The smell of continuing hope
Seek – The particulars of promises
Seize – This opportunity to be yourself
For isolation – devoted
Will be a loyal companion
The emptiness around you
– your truest fan
Relish this one fact
Talent – distinguished –
Will be your greatest symbol
Therefore, nothing is ever wasted space

Tamed

Tamed
    unbelievably dull

Unexciting

So disciplined

    Controlled

        Lifeless

A routine player

    Trained to obey

    Trapped by old ways

    Predictable

        a follower

    Needless to say

        what a cliché

    Grow a backbone

        Find *you!*

Lady Melanie Ann Marie Elizabeth Greenwood

Tell

Her facial expression
 — tells

The emotion in her eyes
 — should tell

Her trembling lips
 — should tell

Her lack of breath
 — should tell

Her raised eye brows
 — should tell

Her pale cheeks
 — should tell

Her unspoken pain
 — should tell

You do not pay attention

That is why
 — you cannot tell

Timid

I find the night
    tames my timid heart

Frees me from
    my unadventurous self

My inability fades
    with the setting of the sun

At night
    I am alive

Free to explore
    the different sides of myself

To become

    Caution then eludes me

My modesty
    bids good night

As I leave the daylight
    to go swimming
        naked in the night

        My vision widens
        My body tingles
        My heart fills
            with gratitude

For a moment
    I have this feeling
        of a great explorer

Lady Melanie Ann Marie Elizabeth Greenwood

So…
    I explore
        losing myself
            becoming myself
                until the moon sets
                    and the dawn
                        returns me
                            to my timid self

But I wait…
        patiently

To become
        that great explorer
            once again

The Artist

A golden frame
On a plain white canvas
May not possess true beauty
But through her eyes – an artist's eyes
May hold endless possibilities

To take a brush
An ordinary brush
And emulate what God has created
Is a gift of grace
That can capture both
Past and present

But to see her paintings
Is to see the artist
And what she has created
Not just a reflection
But an original masterpiece

So…
I consider myself as lucky
As anyone could be
For the day she takes her brush
To paint me the way God sees me
Is the day I know this artist
Will make a legend out of me

Lady Melanie Ann Marie Elizabeth Greenwood

The Engagement

You are my destiny
My Everything
Beloved
Honor me eternally
My Woman
  My Wife
     My Life
Your husband
  I wish to be

The Game

Like a holiday
Family and friends
Gathering together in cheers
Celebrating their favorite teams
Friendly competitions, here and there
With high hopes for each winning team
But nothing beats a great game like the holidays
Filled with smiling faces and wonderful cheers

Lady Melanie Ann Marie Elizabeth Greenwood

The Heart of One

I would rather have won
The heart of one
Than to have won
The heart of many

For it is the many
That would destroy me
And the one
That would die for me

The Light

I wonder if she knows inside
How truly blessed she is
She has this amazing light that glows
Right off her beautiful skin
And when she smiles
Her light glows more

It sets your heart at peace
To know that in this cruel world
A few lights still brightly shine
I promise to pray each night

Should darkness try to dim
This beautiful light
Which will teach each soul
How to truly sing
But you have shown me
I need not worry
For this woman I see
For you have sent your strongest wings
To keep her bright light free

Lady Melanie Ann Marie Elizabeth Greenwood

The Meaning Of Christmas

A time to let go…
for new memories to grow!
To believe in wishes…
of the white – bearded man.
It's a time when reality…
no longer exists.
And the beauty of the invisible …
can really exist.
It is when the children in us…
remember our dreams.
Filled with gifts of…
hopeful possibilities.
Santa and his Reindeer…
are no longer a dream.
Time becomes still…
as sounds find their silence.
Each eye staring…
at the hands of father time.
For at the stroke of midnight,
miracles happen.
And we become children…
once again!
So, the true meaning of Christmas,
that one special day,
when dreams are remembered…
and possibilities…
reborn!

The Poem of Sorrow

It's a quite sense of compilations
Defeated years stacked like staircases in reverse
Disappointment is the permanent designer of my footwear
I'm shocked by my constant surprise
– hope lifted
– hope dies
– hope lifted
– hope dies
Building blocks that have now withered with time
Yet, still I'm judged before I arrive
Yes – there are constant thoughts of suicide
Truth – aged and wise
Battling on – on my behalf to keep me alive
Even though no one ever stands to defend my side
Visited by silence – my old friend
While betrayal stumbles in, drunk as hell,
Demanding memories to show themselves
Tears still close the night for me
At dawn, prayers are squashed beneath bended knees
With faith abandoned – now behind me
Secretly, now and then...
I remember that girl
who once believed
– in God and his promises

Lady Melanie Ann Marie Elizabeth Greenwood

The Seasons

Winter...
        discovering self

Spring...
        exploring new things

Summer...
        filled with laughter

Fall...
        a time to remember

True Love

There you are…
Solace of my heart's journey
The very essence of stellar beauty
Soft in your warmth
Branding my very existence
With your wordless presence
My heart thrums
Forgetting the required beats
Needed for life itself
My adoration intertwines
With your tenderness
Bound
By unbreakable chains of devotion
I would suffer
The scorching flames of a burning sun
If it meant my ashes became
Your most precious possession
And the heavens would find me smiling
I am filled with a calming wonder
Infatuated by the sweetness
Of your charm
I am a reckless decision
Yet a slave to my dependability
You have robbed me
Of my very self
Where now – only true love – sits in its place

Lady Melanie Ann Marie Elizabeth Greenwood

Unique

Remarkable a thing
– should unconsciously demand
of us – attention
Our awareness – like a thief in the night
– stolen from sight
Boldly declaring – remarkable of flavors
Taste deceiving –
With an onslaught of paradise
Deflecting enrapture – with certainty
Our fortress – built in limbo
Surely – worth enduring
For the strongest of desire
Is it not - unique

Virgin

Poetry – I find
Writes itself around you
The virgin expression?
– I'm amused

Vision*

Locked away –
In the deepest parts of me
Are pieces of you –
Safely hidden from view

Your voice –
A melody of sweet caress
Gentle harmonious whispers
A delightful pleasure –
Before my eyes meet rest

Your fragrant smile –
Is the only perfume I wear
Your gentleness – I know not yet
I patiently await embrace

Breathless are my thoughts –
Satisfied by only you
The dearest of all gifts known to me
Is the day my eyes met you

My vision misplaced your unforgettable face
But my heart – forevermore
Will hold you in its place

---

* Dedicated to my Mr. Chicago.

Voluptuous

I am the future –

Attractive
Curvaceous
Desirable
Healthy
Sensual
Well-Endowed

I am the future of
 – Voluptuous Women

Walk

I walked around today
– Lost –
Not knowing who I am
– Questioning –
Everything around me
That I created
Wanting to know why
I was walking
Completely not there
Imagine that
But – I walked
And it was good

Wedding Bells
The Invitation

Wedding bells sounding
Echoing the unity of love
A journey beginning
With a celebration
Commemorating a man and a woman
Becoming husband and wife

Be our guest
At the exchanging of vows
As we take our first step into forever
Beneath the echoing sounds
Of wedding bells

Wheelchair

Every day I watch you
As you wheel across my path
Your troubles seem non-existent
And your spirit untarnished by life

Your patience of others follows
Their lack of understanding
And your courage in the face of danger
Carries with it no doubt

Your joy and laughter is contagious
And your leadership in hope shows strength
A task for you always effortless
For you exhaustion gentle hides itself

I often wondered what kept you going
Until the day I finally asked
Your reply was simply keep looking
One day you will understand

Then I suddenly realized above it all
It was me who kept you going
You were showing me
My patience, my strength, my courage
All the things I'd given up on
Until you embraced my life

Will You Stay

For a time
You dwelled
Belonging only to me

– You stayed

Every moment counted
The collection of memories
Lay in the photos
That time was forbidden to touch

– You stayed

Each room
Filled with echoing words,
Songs, laughter, tears, silence
Stories of you and me

– You stayed

You have always
Stayed with me

Let me
– Stay with you

Wings of Faith

From where I stand
Beauty lies and wishes find their way
To the ears of us
Who have left this world
On destiny's wings of faith

And I believe in things I see
The strength you carry of me
With every tear I feel your pain
And the love you have for me

But the time has come
And I share with you
Through these words of grace
To give you hope but most all
To say your Destiny awaits
That I still see the laughter
And the joys we have shared
Over the years gone by
It is my certainty that you will have
Quite an amazing life

So look for the dreams
You carry deep
Within your heart
And take the journey
With your head up high
And drop a rose bud
For every trail you leave behind
Then I will know that my love
And my wish found its way to you

…Sisters make the best of friends

…I believe in you

You Are...*

I wonder where
This life of mine began
Exactly where
I predicted in time
That luck would find me
Standing here
A part of such
Incredible beings
At last I see
Beyond my dreams
I can't believe
That this is real
...This is real

You are my sunshine
In the morning when I wake
You are the moonlight
That puts the night to rest
You are the warm whispers
Of good within the human race
You are the hands
I depend on to know myself
You are my never-ending star

At last
The mirror's reflection
Shows the real me
The walls no longer
Linger within me
I am free to enjoy
The life I see before me
No more running to find
What is unreal
You fought and found
This beautiful girl you see
All because

Lady Melanie Ann Marie Elizabeth Greenwood

words — Epic Poems of a Poetess

You never gave up on me
My world is complete
I am free

You are my sunshine
In the morning when I wake
You are the moonlight
That puts the night to rest
You are the warm whispers
Of good within the human race
You are the hands
I depend on to know myself
You are my never-ending star

Your light
So bright
It shines through me

* Dedicated to my life's cheerleaders and to Amy Harnell and Brandon Wilde whose musical talent created the song – Never Ending Star.

𝕭𝖔𝖓𝖚𝖘 𝕻𝖔𝖊𝖒𝖘
(Dedications)

Please visit Wikipedia® (The Free Encyclopedia) to learn more about these incredible individuals: www.wikipedia.com

Brave

Dedicated to Mother Teresa

Turmoil
Devastation
Betrayal
Regret
– BRAVE

Unfaithfulness
Filth
Rape
Killing
– BRAVE

Treats
Fear
Drugs
Homelessness
– BRAVE

Wars and Broken Promises
Yet – YOU remain BRAVE

Love – Caring
Devotion – Commitment
Persistence – Purpose
Above all – FAITHFULNESS

It took returning home
To meet you
MAGNIFICENTLY – in the quiet space of a modest garden
Within my Church
      – Where I learned to be BRAVE

Forever — A Letter

Dedicated to Princess Diana

A little too late…

I'd like to say
I didn't waste any time
On idle things

That I'd written my letter to you
As I'd once promised
Along with other things

That I'd mailed it
As originally planned
That I'd fondly waited
For your joyful reply

I'd like to say – my letter
Left you overwhelmed with joy
I'd like to say
That your response
Remained to this day
Delicately framed
On my wall

I'd like to say
I wasn't running late – not at all
To say that I believed you'd
Be around for quite a while
And that the tapping
On my conscious – I'd ignored
But my wall of guilt
Woke me from it all

That now I'm writing
To atone – My Adoration
You will forever know

Lady Melanie Ann Marie Elizabeth Greenwood

Memories of Me

Dedicated to Sergei Grinkov*

I love the way she reminds you of me
Our daughter
Still gentleness
Warm love
Beautiful words spoken
Memories of me
Within the space
Between you and where I stand
Your love sparkles
The brightest star
Meant only for me
Where my soul knows you
It has carried me here
– to my family
Where love is welcomed
Memories live
Where I see you
My wife
My daughter
  – your Sergei

---

* Sergei Grinkov (February 4, 1967 – November 20, 1995) was a Russian pair skater who, with his wife, Ekaterina Gordeeva, won two Olympic Gold Medals.

Pennies

Dedicated to the Penny*

Everyday...What do you see, hear, touch, taste and smell? What do you feel?

Do you realize...That yesterday you saved one hundred lives with the smile on your face?

Do you realize...That the one hundred pennies you found over the course of three months were a gift from one hundred people?

Do you realize...That the perfect bag of red apples you bought for ninety-nine cents was free (remembering the gift of 100 pennies)?

Do you realize...The person you bought your perfect bag of red apples from – added one penny (he found) – to that ninety-nine cents. Then, deposited that one dollar into his child's college fund, because she dreams of being a doctor who will save many lives one day, and every penny counts.

Do you realize...The person you gave your last penny to was able to use it as a tool to un-jam a disk, stuck in his computer, that his boss needed to close a deal. Saving both their jobs.

Do you realize...That disk contained a valuable, creative idea on how to bring clean water to over one billion people?

So, you should be smiling, because these are the stories we tell – **the positive truths.**

Remembering...The tiniest deed that begins with a positive act – has the greatest impact.

* To the Penny – Worldwide.

Lady Melanie Ann Marie Elizabeth Greenwood

Remember Me

Dedicated to Selena

¿Me recuerdas?
  – Do you remember me?
Estoy aquí
  – I'm here
Recuerdo
  – Remembering you
Recordar nos
  – Remembering us
Juntos
  – Together

Recordarme!
  – Remember Me!

Voy para siempre
  – I will forever
Recuerden
  – Remember you
En la quietud
  – In the stillness
De susurros olvidados
  – Of forgotten whispers

Singing – Te Amo

Shadow

Dedicated to Michael Jackson

Michael – My Michael
How I have hidden in your shadow
My shyness comforted
For I was never alone

Now
Exposed
Hopelessness is left in the wake of desperation
No longer am I able to clothe myself
I am cold
Bittersweet are my steps forward
Did you not realize
Forevermore
Your promise that I would never be alone

My saddened heart aches
In realization of my selfishness
For every sweet word of yours
I make my own
My broken heart – renewed
The sweetness of your memory
Your message – transforming me

Now I stand brave

Michael – My Michael
Hidden in my shadow
I find you whispering
That I am not alone
You are here with me

The Towers

Dedicated to the Heroes of WTC 9/11

Another night has come and gone
As dawn approaches near
Creeping slowly upon the horizon
To brighten a brand new day

With rays of light
Spread widely across the sky
Memories flood my mind
Of a once great skyline

Where simple people
Like you and me
From every walk of life
Would roam the halls at daybreak
Until the sun faded into night

And while we slept
The doves took rest
Upon its sacred walls
As the night awaited
The coming of the dawn
What a day unfolded
Placed a nation in despair
Flames burned…Innocents lost
Lives changed
— Forever

But in the end, we stood united
Burning little flames of hope
Through the dawn
For our heroes
Whose gentle souls we remember

So close your eyes
For just a moment
And look deep within
You can still see the doves resting
Upon sacred walls.

Within My Touch

Dedicated to Helen Keller

My hands may seem like simple things
> But for me
>> they are my world

They are what I use
> to see and speak
>> And what I need
>>> to hear

I count on them
> to guide my way
>> As I take
>>> my steps through life

With every touch
> I have learned
>> of beauty, hope and love

But…
> I have also learned of other things

And…
> of how the world sees me

So even though
> I am not like you
>> My eyes won't see
>>> My ears won't hear
>>>> My lips won't move to speak

I see the world
> with clarity
>> I hear the world
>>> loudly

And…
> my voice speaks through movements

Lady Melanie Ann Marie Elizabeth Greenwood

Within my touch
> lives my life
>> And in it
>>> my uniqueness

words — Epic Poems of a Poetess

Discover the Artist Within You

For Your Notes

words — Epic Poems of a Poetess

For Your Masterpiece

For Your Notes

For Your Masterpiece

 # For Your Notes

For Your Masterpiece

For Your Notes

For Your Masterpiece

Special Note of Gratitude
Written by the Poetess

This journey has been one of discovery and breaking through barriers I never knew existed within myself. Learning about them has truly been pure joy.

Therefore, I cannot figure out whether my discovery is captivating or
just simply captivity.
But writing tames my heart, caresses my journey with this mark of love.
I have become a story in itself.
One, where I am the sole keeper of this precious key — called my life.
But, it is remembrance, this theater that consoles my soul.
For I am grateful that history lends itself to me,
I often find I am lost in its memories.
However, thrilled that I am allowed so confidently to express myself.
Where words are the very things I yearn for
the way men and women yearn for that never-ending romance.
I cannot image a life where my outer world has no letters,
No words that I could create and manipulate, making them my very own.
When it comes to words – I am selfish.
I feel no shame in this admittance.
I realize now my in-depth appreciation can only find itself devoted to a universe
filled with possibilities.
Requiring great understanding and great knowledge.
I have still to discover more of its endless beauty and power.
And truly, I am OK with that being said.
Maybe in some distant future, history will once again lend itself to me,
and grace me with the presence of its greatest Artist,
or anyone it seems fitting to bestow upon me these blessings.
To admit my conceit in saying _maybe_ in a past life I sat with giants,
I would gracefully accept.
Indeed, I would have had it no other way.
Without any detailed explanation, I can honestly say,
I truly have all that I have ever desired.
My ink, my quill, a plain white flawless sheet of paper,
with its endless possibilities and unlimited space.
But above all, my wild imagination, which I take great pleasure in exploring on a
daily basis.
It would seem that happiness and harmony have found their way to me.
Within it – my freedom as well!
I guess my teachers were right after all.

I truly am – a great lover of words.
Maybe – a day will find me writing a great book that will either *<u>enlighten</u>* the world
<u>or not</u>.
But then, greatness was never accomplished in trying to please anyone.
Either way, I am certain my humility will get the best of me.
But, I can finally say with great certainty, with a gigantic smile on my face,
That finally – ***I am free.***

Lady Melanie Ann Marie Elizabeth Greenwood

About the Poetess

Born in Belize, Central America, to a military family, she spent a few years in England, with summer vacations in the United States. In 1985, she moved to America, with her mother and sister, and has been here ever since, residing primarily in New Jersey.

Her work has won numerous awards, including the The Prometheus Muse of Fire Award, the Poet of the Year Medallion, and the Shakespeare Trophy of Excellence through The Famous Poets Society. Her poems have also been published in several anthologies.

With an entrepreneur mindset, she decided to found Zillionaires Publishing, L.L.C., to publish Words - Epic Poems of a Poetess, her first book of poetry. Currently, she is working on her first novel, called Forevermore - A Love Story, coming 2013.

While she has many areas of interest – particularly traveling and learning new cultures – one of her greatest joys is inspiring others. "Ill-literacy" in the world today is her biggest concern and therefore, she intends to volunteer in support for change.

The Remarkable Worldwide Puzzle Board
Written by the Poetess

I have worked in the corporate world for many years and, within the offices and cubicles, I have met, a poet, an author, a writer, a doctor, a scientist, an interior designer, an architect, an astronaut, a jeweler, a fashion designer, a model, a school-teacher, a firefighter, an actor, a personal trainer, a gymnast, a ballerina, a film producer, an athlete, an educator, an artist, a photographer, a visionary, a philanthropist, a singer, a builder, an historian, inspirational speakers, many advocates and promising leaders. I have met them all. And every time I'd see them or shake their hands, I'd always wonder, what I could do to inspire them to become what they were truly destined to be.

One day, I stood up in my cubicle, looking at everything within it and around it – and although I was grateful for the opportunity – I decided that I no longer wanted to be a part of a puzzle with pieces scattered from their rightful places. So, I began learning about all those who had laid the foundation before me. Those who'd found their rightful place on this worldwide puzzle board. I learned about their failures, their determinations, and their triumphs. What inspired them, who inspired them, or what finally forced them to follow their destined path. I studied those who received help from others, those who were laughed out the doors for their ideas, and those who did it all on their own. But ultimately and most importantly, I dug deep for the clues they left that would inspire me. And smiled with myself, when I found them.

> *When someone tells you "No," – thank them and move on to the next, and keep moving on to the next and the next until you find your "Yes." Even if, after you've made a complete circle, you find that that "Yes" is coming from the person in the very spot you are standing on – from you – and you find that you have to create it yourself, you would have found your "Yes."*

So, I learned, I read, I re-organized and I intentionally placed myself – even at times – forced myself – near those few individual's I knew would encourage and inspire me. Needless to say, I'd found my "Yes." And yes – it did come from the person in that very same spot where I was standing. Oh, and I did remember to say thank you to everyone who had told me "No."

I find I catch myself every now and then looking back, but not for the reasons you would think. Where I once sat, – now sits an empty cubicle. I don't believe anyone has filled it yet. I actually hope no one does, except for the person whose true piece of the puzzle it is to fit that spot.

And yes, there are still obstacles that tend to get in the way, but now I know, that those obstacles are just the scattered pieces of others trying the find their rightful place on this worldwide puzzle board. And so, you give them a little nudge in the form of inspiration and encouragement to help them along their way, and so on and so on. And sometimes you may come across an obstacle that tends to be a little bit stubborn. Wanting to push you out of your rightful place, for whatever reason. Those times become the opportunity to learn patience, understanding, and discover the power within you to hold your own.

I am forever changed. And from where I sit – fitting nicely into my piece of the puzzle – I look forward to inspiring and encouraging others to find their rightful place on this extraordinary worldwide puzzle board. And this book – I believe – is the product of what **can be** created when you have an idea and when you team up with those who have found their rightful place: The Poet, The Writer, The Designer, The Editor, The Photographer, The Web Designer, The Printer, The Event Planner, The Attorney, The Family, The Friends, The Encouragers, and so on and so on. Leaving a piece of history – becoming the inspiration.

And that is what I learned about what I could do to inspire others to become what they were truly destined to be. And in turn, they could do the same. Like those before me, who inspired me. I thank you. I believe Michael Jackson said it best with "The Man in the Mirror." For truly, if you do want to make this world a better place, who better to start with than yourself.

Lady Melanie Ann Marie Elizabeth Greenwood

words — Epic Poems of a Poetess

𝔄 𝔖𝔭𝔢𝔠𝔦𝔞𝔩 𝔗𝔯𝔢𝔞𝔱

Here is a glimpse of my upcoming novel…

FOREVERMORE
A Love Story

Written by: Melanie Greenwood

The following is a work of fiction. Names, characters, places and incidents are products of the author's imagination or are used fictitiously and are not to be construed as real. Any resemblance to actual events, locales, organizations, or persons, living or dead, is entirely coincidental.

Lady Melanie Ann Marie Elizabeth Greenwood

Chapter I

Waiting was never really my forte. It was the one thing I'd never managed to build into my character over the years. I simply had no patience for it. I was a stickler for the rules. If you say you are going to do something, then you should do it. If you say you are going to be somewhere, then be there. I hated waiting. And oddly enough, here I was, doing the very thing I hated.

I checked my cell phone again – nothing!

No text. No calls. No messages. My plane landed three-and-a-half hours ago. My butt, beyond numb and oddly burning! I assumed the scorching sun had something to do with it. Any other explanation was just too scary to entertain.

It had to be over a hundred degrees.

Not a cloud in sight to momentarily hide the blazing sun. I couldn't believe I hadn't already drowned in a pool of my own sweat.

The light breeze blowing did nothing to cool the heat that had already engulfed me. Like a very large fan on low, blowing only heat, roasting my skin as it blew by.

"Was every day in Mexico like this?" I questioned.

"Oh! Don't be silly Martin, of course it is." I corrected myself.

Taxi's drove by me, one after another, as I sat on an iron bench outside the terminal. The temptation just to get into the air-conditioned cab was seriously overpowering my will to keep my word. Which was the only thing keeping me here… the fact that I'd never intentionally broken a promise in my life.

But that was slowly about to change.

Bored, I looked around. It seemed that just about everyone was waiting behind the glass walls of the air-conditioned airport. I was the only buffoon sitting outside. Besides a few locals, who were already immune to this kind of heat and humidity.

"Despite Noel Coward's marvelous lyrics, "Mad dogs and Englishmen go out in the noonday sun…something, something," I thought. My half Brazilian heritage – at the moment – did nothing for me. This kind of capital punishment one was willing to cause oneself was just…

"What's this?" My brain screamed out interrupting my train of thought.

"Yum-Yum," I smiled.

"A treat," I told myself.

Pleased. I suddenly found my apparent foolishness and discomfort being highly rewarded by the most exquisite creature. My impatience suddenly overshadowed by her appearance.

My heart soared. She was magnificent.

"A Ray of Sunshine," my heart told my brain. An interesting thought, considering a moment ago, the last thing I wanted was more sunshine.

"And refreshingly beautiful," it added.

Although she was short, maybe five-five, five-six, if I had to guess – she walked with her head held high, showing great poise.

Her complexion was that of a golden sun goddess. My brain quickly flipped through an old art history book of goddesses to see which goddess had escaped those pages.

Her smile. "Aw...her smile," I thought, was hypnotizing.

"Yes," I admitted, agreeing with myself.

And white sparkling teeth. "Nice."

"It was days like this that I was grateful for my 20/20 vision." My gratitude took on the form of an appreciative smile.

Focused now on her hair.

Her honey-blond hair – thick, long and wavy – probably saw more visits to the beauty salon than a supermodel's. Good God, a man could easily get lost in all that hair. I concluded.

It wasn't hard to guess that the color of her eyes were blue.

I imagined. Light blue, I hoped, because it was my favorite color. The kind of blue at the shallow end of the ocean before you knew you were heading into deeper waters. And boy, I urgently wanted to drown myself in deeper waters. Releasing a deep breath, my appreciative smile deepened.

With the sun shining directly on an already glowing face, I realized she couldn't have been older than eighteen or nineteen. Yet, with the sun illuminating her voluptuous curves, her body said otherwise of her age.

A woman.

Her laced white sundress flowed over her the way a pillow fits over a pillowcase. "Hahaha," I chuckled at use of this unusual analogy. This is bad.

I shook my head in disbelief. "But, how in god's name do you describe perfection?"

Looking down, I noticed she was shoeless.

Bare feet and in this heat! "How in god's name..." my thought stopped itself. For someone who didn't believe in god, I was sure using the man's name quite a bit.

"Oh well!" It didn't matter. It was the perfect excuse to buy her several hundred pairs of Gucci and Prada. After all, for her, only designers would do.

I smiled again with images running through my head of her trying on each pair.

As my eyes continued to explore, I pleasantly noticed the long split on each side of her dress. Both emotions – delight and jealousy – slammed into me.

Memories of my mum flooded my mind. "So I became paternal!" as she would say.

"Where is her father?" her voice echoed in my head.

"A respectful young lady should not undermine herself this way," I imagined her saying and smiled, recalling the many stories I'd overheard, eavesdropping on her and her sister, my aunt Olivia. Speaking about their youth, hiding from their mother and

words — Epic Poems of a Poetess

wearing not-so-lady like clothing themselves.

Out of respect, I allowed my eyes to drift to her beautiful hair. But that only lasted a few seconds.

"Shame, shame, shame...on me." I scolded myself.

Laughing, I straightened myself after realizing my head was leaning partially to the left along with the direction the light breeze was blowing her dress.

Once again, out of respect and using greater determination this time, I imagined what her voice would sound like. Soft, tender. Gentle, with the hum of a whisper. Soothing. Or, maybe bright and alive!

But, whatever it sounded like, I was sure, like the rest of her, it was perfect.

I slipped into another world, refusing to release her soft, gentle and reassuring appearance.

"A woman. No, a young lady," I corrected myself.

"Wouldn't a young lady like this have to have someone equally beautiful as her boyfriend?" I wondered.

"The Captain of the soccer team, tennis team or the swimming team." Jealousy slammed into me again.

"Maybe none of the above," I told myself, to tame my jealousy and quickly assumed she had an overprotective father instead.

"Yes!" I smiled willfully.

"An overprotective father," because I'd never met one who didn't like me and encouraged marriage after the first conversation.

"Indeed." My jealousy subsided.

After a while of quietly enjoying the view, I noticed something peculiar. Besides the fact that she hadn't stop smiling from the moment I laid eyes on her, she was touching the hands of every person that passed her by.

"What an oddity."

I could feel my forehead furrow, as my brain searched for a sane answer to her peculiar behavior.

But mid-thought, I was rudely interrupted by the foulest smell.

Painfully, my eye was forced to follow my wrinkled nose to this distasteful scent.

I can't say the beggar who suddenly decided to grace me with his presence surprised me. He reeked of alcohol and having forgotten that a bath was a necessary part of being human. That was the thing about addictions; they drowned out your humanity.

No introduction was necessary.

Open palm, bloodshot eyes, caveman teeth, severely chapped lips, receding hairline, a face that was badly burnt and peeling and a smile that truly left me uncomfortable. Like any other beggar I'd met, he needed money to entertain his addiction. I took out my wallet and gave him five thousand Mexican pesos. I told him in Spanish to get himself a hotel. But I knew it was hopeless. Normally, I would set them up in a hotel for a few days myself and, while they lived like a king, I would get them the help they desperately needed. But, with this guy, the stench was so bad, I almost keeled over from the lack of personal hygiene mixed in with the heat and humidity. And by the looks and obvious smell, I'd say he was on his way out of this life anyway.

I wasn't sure if it was my foul neighbor or the fact that my ray of sunshine was nowhere in sight, but the sudden exhaustion I thought I'd escaped earlier was suddenly starting to resurface.

Four days of traveling. Endless hours crammed into coach because first-class was sold out and I was desperate – broken up by endless hours waiting in airports, due to cancelled flights between New Zealand, Australia, Japan, Miami and Mexico. I suddenly found myself questioning my career choice.

Right now, being a freelance photographer and writer didn't look so appealing. Maybe I was just burnt out. It felt as if I'd already been in every country in the world on more than one occasion, with the exception of Mexico – until now. And as much as I didn't want to think about it – especially with the current heat and humidity – maybe all I needed was a nice lukewarm bath and a week of sleep to recover my perspective and sense of appreciation. After all – unlike most people – I was very lucky to have traveled to so many beautiful places, though there were definitely a few I would rather altogether forget.

Thinking of this, I found my mind pleasantly drifting to the happy memories of the families I'd stayed with over the years and the good friends I'd met along the way.

For a moment, I wondered what my new Mexican family would be like.

According to my friend Genevieve, this was Manuel's first time accepting this type of living arrangement. At first, he was a bit put off by having a complete stranger taking up room and board with him and his family. But Genevieve had assured him that I could be fully trusted. It also didn't hurt having outstanding references. And my previous conversation with him sounded promising. Though I'd never gotten around to asking Genevieve how she and Manuel had been acquainted.

I'd explained to him that I'd found the room and board experience rewarding and that I was always lucky to have had great referrals from friends, who'd stayed at a home and fell in love with their hosts, their culture and the hospitality. So, these families looked forward to their next guest, and the money they received was well worth the effort. But, because I was always a bit more generous, my name was well known and I constantly received letters welcoming me back with open arms.

Then I briefly explained my acquaintance with Genevieve. Which at the time had worked out pretty well. Because not only did I room and board with her and her family, but she was my assignment, as well. The marine biologist and her underwater exhibition to save the Blue Hole and the Barrier Reef in Belize. She was actually quite taken with the country itself. She loved Belize and so did I.

That assignment had lasted a little shy of two years. But, I assured Manuel that the assignment I was doing would only require me to stay three to four months tops, and that it was actually a favor to Genevieve – for a friend of hers.

I just needed to gather information and some photos for the daughter of a memoir author who wanted to complete the unfinished manuscript she'd found several months after her mother's death. And so, I was looking forward to this new adventure, exploring Mexico and making new friends.

I looked at my watch – it was now a little past three.

Restless and exhausted, I suddenly found I could breathe again. My foul neighbor was gone.

Sucking in a few additional quick breaths, I stood up and stretched my six-foot athletic frame with a loud moan. For a twenty-one year old, I felt old.

"Four years of traveling will do that to a man." I thought absentmindedly. Having traveled two out of the four years with a few of my father's good friends. Who enjoyed having me as their new apprentice.

My stomach growled. "Great!" I was hungry too now.

Yawning, I rubbed my face and then removed my cell phone from my pants pocket. Having found Manual's number, I sat down and pressed talk.

With the phone set at my ear and ringing, I looked up and my heart sank.

My restlessness, exhaustion and hunger subsided. "Hola!" I didn't answer but instead immediately pressed the End button on the gentle voice that answered hello in Spanish. My ray of sunshine had reappeared and demanded my complete attention.

My cell phone rang but I ignored the call.

The beep that followed, however, confirmed they'd left a message. But I was occupied. Drooling was a better term.

"This girl was perfect!"

My mind wandered to the many beautiful women I'd met over the years, but none captivated me the way she did. To such a degree that mentally, I went from being a twenty-one year old to a thirteen year old, love–sick pup in seconds.

I needed to know her name.

"What's your name?" I whispered. Knowing full well she couldn't hear me. Or, could she?

My eyes widened suddenly with shock when she looked right at me, at the same time touching the hand of the foul man, as he was passing by.

He stopped.

His hand entwined with hers. My nose wrinkled in disgust. They were both looking my way.

I quickly pretended to scratch my forehead, while peeking at them through the spaces between my fingers.

They turned and looked at each other.

He smiled at her, released her hand, then walked away. She glanced at me once more then turned her head and continued walking. Smiling as she went along on her merry way.

"What was that about?" I wondered.

But after a while my mind gave up searching for an answer. She never looked my way again. And, I simply returned to being a lovesick pup.

The sudden urge to throw a kiss her way came as no shock to me.

"Amore!" My mum's voice popped into my mind again, along with the memory of my birthday.

I was seven. The music that played in the background was Enya's "Marble Halls." A favorite of hers!

"Ask her to dance," she'd encouraged me.

I don't remember how I'd quite made it over to Sophia. The only thing I remembered was standing in front of her. My right hand behind my back and my left hand hanging at my side. Trembling.

My eyes widened in shock when she leaned over to kiss my right cheek. I remembered all the blood, in my body, wasted no time rushing to my face. But, the world's biggest blush didn't matter I was always to be a gentleman. It was expected of me.

What was not expected – due to her unexpected affection – was that I'd lost my voice and my lunch over her pretty baby blue dress.

"Eeww!"

Smack! She slapped my left cheek.

That was the first time anyone had ever kissed me and slapped me in the same second.

I remember turning to look at my mum in shock. My left hand cupped the slap mark on my left cheek and my right hand cupped the soft, gentle kiss on my right cheek.

My mum had the most beautiful smile on her face and her arms opened wide, welcoming me.

She never took her eyes off me as I ran up to her and away from Sophia.

I threw myself into her opened arms. As she carried me, I whispered…

"She hates me and she loves me."

My mum replied, "Amore!" Shaking her head and whisking me onto the dance floor for the dance I'd never had with Sophia.

Sophia and her mum left my birthday party right after. My mum had to replace Sophia's very expensive baby blue dress, and the love she and I shared never blossomed into anything more than friendship. That day was my first taste of the silly things we do when we think we're in love.

I laughed at the memory.

But as men, I don't think that sort of sillyness is something we ever outgrow. Because the urge to throw a kiss her way only became stronger!

Goodness, Martin! I took in a deep breath hoping to clear my mind. Get a grip! But it was useless. My common sense completely abandoned me. And with the amount of traveling I've done, what a coincidence that the movie I saw on my most recent flight was "The Mask" with Jim Carrey. His wolfman scene with Cameron

Diaz flashed fresh in my mind. Then, forgetting where I was, my lips slowly puckered in formation for the kiss.

"Ah! I wouldn't do that if I were you." A familiar, gentle voice whispered calmly next to me.

I froze. My lips still puckered halfway in front of me.

"You might need this for the drool," he continued, as he placed a white handkerchief in front of my face.

Still frozen, my mind wandered to the voice I'd hung up on earlier. I knew it wasn't Manuel. His voice definitely lacked gentleness. Nevertheless, I was still in shock.

I somehow managed to slowly retract my lips to their normal form, with my eyes slowly moving far right to see the face that had caught my sudden and irrational behavior.

When my eyes couldn't move any further, my head somehow managed a slight turn in the same direction. He was young. His face was turned away from mine. He was looking at my ray of sunshine. Jealousy resurfaced. Like a madman, screaming to get rid of the competition! But I ignored it. Figuring one irrational act was my quota for today.

Ignoring my inner turmoil and purposely keeping my eyes away from her, I focused on him instead, noticing his flawless tan. His skin was wrinkle free. Unlike the foul man he definitely used sunscreen. His lip had a natural pout and his nose was perfectly proportioned. From what I could tell by his profile, it suited his slender face and high cheekbone. His hair was wavy and short. Jet-black. Ear a normal size. That's assuming the other was the same. And he seemed to have an athletic build.

I took a quick guess at his age. Seventeen.

Catching me off guard, he turned toward me as I was staring at him.

Awkward! I blinked my eyelids several times, pretending to get something out of my eye.

"You're a little on the weird side, aren't you?" he asked. His expression worried.

Well, that attempt obviously failed miserably.

But when I looked at him again, his face was filled with humor. Deep dimples, teeth sparkling white and perfect with a smile from ear to ear.

He shook his head releasing a breath, "Yep! She'll do that to you." he said, looking at me, then at her and back to me.

Reminding me about the handkerchief with a shake of his hand, I took it from him and wiped my mouth. Which surprisingly had drool. But his smile turned warm and I took that as confirmation that he understood my sudden and irrational behavior. I exhaled with relief.

He extended his hand once again, this time introducing him self. "I'm Philippe." He shook my hand asking, "You must be Martin?"

Shaking his hand, I nodded in agreement, realizing this was one of those moments we'd never forget, and I half smiled.

With my voice finally recovering from its initial frozen shock, I asked in a weak tone, "Where is Manuel?"

He said abruptly releasing my hand. "He had something to do and asked if I could pick you up instead."

But before I could ask who Manuel was in relation to him, he interrupted me.

"Are these you're things?"

I politely smiled and said, "Yes."

As he grabbled my bags, he welcomed me to Mexico with warmth exuding from him.

He loved his country.

He told me to follow him and not to forget my money.

"What money?"

"On the bench." He motioned with his head as he continued to walk away.

I turned to look and sure enough, there it was. Five thousand Mexican pesos held down by a small rock.

"He couldn't have forgotten it," I thought. The small rock assured me of that. I picked up the money, disregarded the rock, and placed it in my pants pocket.

My eyes quickly searched for the foul man, who was gone. And I hoped for one final look at my ray of sunshine, but she was gone, too. My heart sank. I felt a sudden pain. A loss. The thought of never seeing her again left me with a devastating feeling.

But even with the sudden feelings of loss and devastation lingering in my heart, Philippe had made me feel comfortable, welcomed.

Trusting that, I let my guard down, treating him as a longtime friend.

Not thinking, I blurted out as we approached his car, "A Datsun!"

Laughing. "Didn't they stop making these things in the year one?"

"You're a funny man," he said, his expression showing his disapproval of my attempt at a joke.

"I have no problems with you walking," he said only too willingly.

I looked at him my smile immediately vanished.

I dragged my fingers across my now-serious lips, indicating that they were now sealed. While feeling a sense of relief that I hadn't also commented on his white shoes, white pants and bright orange shirt, which made him look like the actors straight out of "Miami Vice." Which I'd recently seen in reruns, late one night, staying at a hotel in Miami due to a cancelled flight.

My peripheral vision caught him looking away as he placed my luggage in the trunk of his car then walked around to the driver's side to open his door. Once opened, he leaned down and a latch clicked.

"I didn't think these cars had that capability," I thought to myself. But I refrained from commenting on that, as well.

Distracted, I guess I didn't hear when he'd said not to open the door, because I pulled the latch and when the door didn't open, I pulled on the latch once again, but this time with definite force and pulled the entire latch off the door.

I chuckled then quickly recovered.

The handle broke right off. I couldn't believe what just happened. I rubbed the bridge of my nose with my left index finger. Then curled my hand into a fist and placed it at my side.

"Ah!" I whispered to myself as I watched Phillippe emerge from the driver's side of the car.

The expression on his face gave away his thoughts.

I immediately realized that tending to foreigners weren't really his favorite pastime and that his politeness when we'd first met was just that, politeness and nothing more. A misjudgment on my part!

He didn't say a word, as he walked over and stood in front of me, his hand opened.

With a sharp, penetrating look, his stare went from my eyes to the latch in my right hand, then to his opened hand, indicating, without a word, to place it in his hand, which I did immediately.

My eyes looked down away from his face.

My head and body followed in the same direction, as utter embarrassment overwhelmed me.

This time, I was sure that if I kept up at this rate, Mexico would become my permanent home. And, for a moment I thought of the guy who had become shark bait in that old "Miami Vice" rerun.

I quickly found myself making sure I didn't have the car jack or some other instrument coming at my head.

But when I didn't see him, my instincts about what I had just thought made me turn around abruptly, only to find he was not even behind me. Which was good.

Once things came into focus again, I saw that quite a lot of people and cars were going about their business, and life had continued to move along nicely, while I had gotten carried away with my own silly thoughts.

Then I heard an annoyed voice yelling in my direction.

"Are you coming or what?"

He was already in the car with the windows rolled down on the passenger side.

I bent over and my eyes met his. His expression was just as annoyed as his voice.

"The door is jammed again, so you'll have to climb in through the window," he said. And through his annoyed expression, I watched as a wicked smile slowly developed.

At which point I didn't dare ask if I could possibly climb through his side of the car to my seat.

As I stared at the small window I had to somehow fit through, I tried to figure out the best possible outcome for this unexpected dilemma I'd somehow managed to get myself into. Until it suddenly dawned on me... didn't I say earlier how I was looking forward to this new adventure and meeting new friends?

Well, my adventure had started a lot sooner than expected.

I stood there in the middle of what seemed like rush hour on a Friday afternoon, with the sun nowhere near setting, still baking in a thousand-degree oven. But I now had to climb through the window of a Datsun and, to make matters worse, walking on my side of the sidewalk, slowly making her way in my direction, was my ray of sunshine.

"Why is she doing that?" I questioned, as I watched her touching the hands of everyone who walked by her. As annoyed as I was at the moment, because I didn't have an answer to this oddity, I realized I was unable to stay annoyed for too long.

She was smiling sweetly.

I felt my entire body go weak with each step she took toward me.

Then, every bone in my body crumbled. I fell slightly into the side of Philippe's car for support. My heart was pounding. A strong, burning heat washed over me, which I knew had nothing to do with the current temperature.

When I attempted to straighten myself out, my foot — caught between the sidewalk and Philippe's car — tripped the edge of the sidewalk and I went crashing down while grabbing the car door for support.

I felt my left ankle twist.

I sucked in a breath and bit my bottom lip to stop the shout stuck in my throat at the pain. And the force with which I fell seemed to have been so powerful that the car door popped open with a loud crack.

Realizing that grabbing the door to break my fall wasn't the brightest idea, nonetheless, relief washed over me, since I no longer had to climb through the window. Either way, it was embarrassing.

Except now, my heart was beating with a different emotion. Fear. If the car door broke off its hinges, shark bait would no longer be a thought. It would be a certainty.

Before I could move my hand off the door, I saw a head slowly peek over it from inside the car. Followed by the expression I was now becoming quite familiar with. Annoyance.

His piercing brown eyes showed no hope of a future friendship between us, his lips forced together to silence whatever vulgarity was at the tip of his tongue.

I didn't say a word. Forgetting the pain I felt throbbing in my left ankle, I had no choice but to wait patiently for whatever would come next.

He burst out laughing.

I was at a loss for words. Shocked. I wasn't sure whether to laugh with him, smile, or just sit there. I decided, for survival's sake, just to sit there.

"Well, I guess you got the door open," he said in a surprised voice that escaped through his uncontrollable laughter.

I glanced away from him for a quick second to look at the door.

"Oh!" I said pretending to be as surprised as he was.

"I guess I did."

But the truth was that I was just happy the door was still attached to the car.

Then I said, sarcastically, "And I was so looking forward to climbing in through the window."

"And I was so looking forward to seeing you do it," he admitted, as disappointment crossed his face.

"But, I'll take the sprained ankle for now," he said, with a quick recovery and a wicked smile.

I frowned in response. But that just made his smile grow even wider.

"Payback is a —" but he interrupted me.

"Are you going to sit there all day or can we really go this time?" he asked, a bit bored.

I gently moved my body slowly around the car door and held onto it. Delicately.

"Now, don't break anything." He jested, looking straight ahead. I looked at him my lips pressed tightly together forming a line.

He turned to look at me. "Oops! Did I say that?" Laughing, he faced forward.

I growled inwardly. "Don't worry, I don't think I'm that clumsy," I replied unamused. Justifying the day I was having due to a lack of sleep.

When I reached for the seatbelt, he extended his right hand to help me and even though I could have used the additional support, I waved my hand shaking him off. I was just too frustrated with him.

"No thanks!" I blurted out not caring if his feelings were hurt. Which I highly doubt they were.

"O-kay!" he said non-chalantly hoping for a guilty effect while slowly pulling his hand away, still smiling.

He placed them on the keys in the ignition and started the car. Then putting the car in drive with his foot pressing down on the breaks.

"Like a tugboat, huh!" I commented with a devilish smile.

He released the breaks and the car jerked forward. "Hey!" I yelled. Pulling my foot from the side of the wheel. He said nothing and just smiled.

I refrained from further sarcasm and biting down on my bottom lip like before except this time, to stop the outburst of laughter wanting to escape at the sound of his old beat-up Datsun.

I gripped the seat belt with my left hand. My right hand still gripping the door gently making sure I didn't break anything on his car and keeping the pressure off my left ankle. I could feel it starting to swell, and throb as if it had its own heartbeat as I hoist myself into the car.

I sighed with relief. I'd made it in safely. Although, I wasn't quite sure how safe that would be. So, I pulled the seat belt over my right arm and stretched it across my waist.

When I tried to clip it in place, I noticed there was nothing to clip it into. I immediately looked up at him. My mouth slightly parted. "Ah?" I started to speak. Then holding back the rest of my statement. Darn car was falling a part. Literally.

Without turning his head, I could see his expression taking on a new emotion. Shame.

Sympathy overwhelmed me as I saw a layer of his veneer crumble.

He was poor but tried to do the best with what he had. I found a new appreciation for him and realized the harm I'd caused with my remark about his car, even though that was never my intention but just a poor attempt at breaking the ice.

Releasing the seat belt, I turned to close the door and saw the gentleness of her soft hand reaching out. She was searching for someone to touch. "How could I have forgotten her?" My heart scowled at my brain.

Without thinking, my heart took over and I just reacted. I reached my hand out to her.

Everything around me stopped. My heart slowed to an impossible beat. My peripheral vision abandoned me. And the built-in adjustable lens of my eyes zoomed in on her hand.

I felt like I was looking though binoculars. Everything else became a blur in the background.

Her fingers were long and slender. Her nails were just the right length, not too long and not too short. They were filed in a square shape. Her silver nail polish sparkled and shined in the sunlight like the New Year's Eve ball in Times Square. Her skin was truly flawless. Youthful. No signs of stress from being overworked. Remarkable!

I imagined the companies that would fall all over themselves, trying to sign her as a spokesperson.

Then, with what now felt like a routine, I forgot where I was. I realized that the last bit of air had left my lungs. With my hand stretching in a desperate attempt to touch her, I stopped breathing and felt them collapse.

My chest cracked.

For a brief moment, all I did was reach.

Reach and reach for her.

"Oh no!" My brain screamed in panic, when my middle finger touched the tip of hers.

"What the–" were the last words I thought, before everything went black.

www.ingramcontent.com/pod-product-compliance
Lightning Source LLC
Chambersburg PA
CBHW032251150426
43195CB00008BA/411